Contents

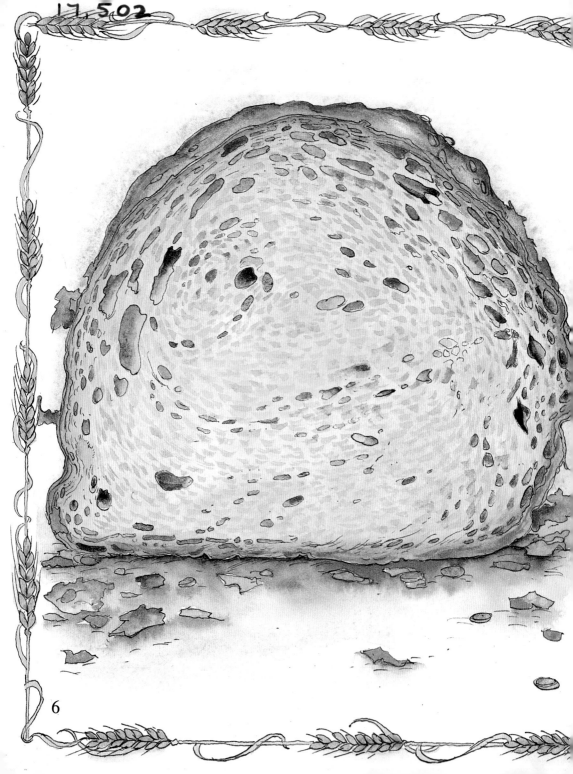

The first bread

Bread has been an important food for thousands of years, and dates back to very early times. In those days, people did not have many machines to help them. They used to grind wheat or millet between two stones to make flour. The flour was then mixed with water and the bread was baked over an open fire.

We know that the Romans had bakeries. In a Roman bakery the grain would first be ground to make flour. Then the bread would be made. It would be sold still fresh and warm over a counter on the street.

Flat bread

Most flat bread is unleavened. This means
that it is cooked without yeast, the special
ingredient that makes bread rise. Unleavened
bread is popular in many countries,
particularly in Pakistan, India, Bangladesh,
Mexico and the Middle East. It is soft and
floppy when it is warm.

Indian flat breads are often cooked in a heavy cast-iron pan called a 'tava'. They may also be cooked in a clay oven called a 'tandoor', or fried in a 'karhai'. In the Middle East bread is often baked over a metal dome on an open fire or in a charcoal oven.

Crisp bread

Matza is a special Jewish unleavened bread
which people eat at Passover. The dough is
rolled out thinly and cooked in a very hot
oven. When it is cooked matza is crisp and
light. It can be stored like a biscuit if it is kept
dry. This is especially useful when cooking is
difficult or not allowed, such as on the Jewish
Sabbath.

Indian poppadoms are crisp and wafer-like.

Bannocks, or Scottish oatcakes, are made of barley flour and soured milk. They can be cooked in a griddle or in the oven.

Leavened bread

The special ingredient of leavened bread is yeast. This makes the bread puff up or rise. The other two main ingredients are flour and water, or sometimes milk. The flour and water are mixed together with the yeast and then kneaded into a firm dough. The dough is put in a warm place so that the yeast inside it can begin to work. The dough is allowed to swell to about twice its original size. It is then kneaded again and allowed to rise once more before being cooked in a hot oven.

Brown and white

Flour can be made from all kinds of cereals, including oats, barley, maize and rye. Most of the flour you see in the shop is made of wheat. Wholemeal flour is made from the whole wheat grain. Brown flour is made

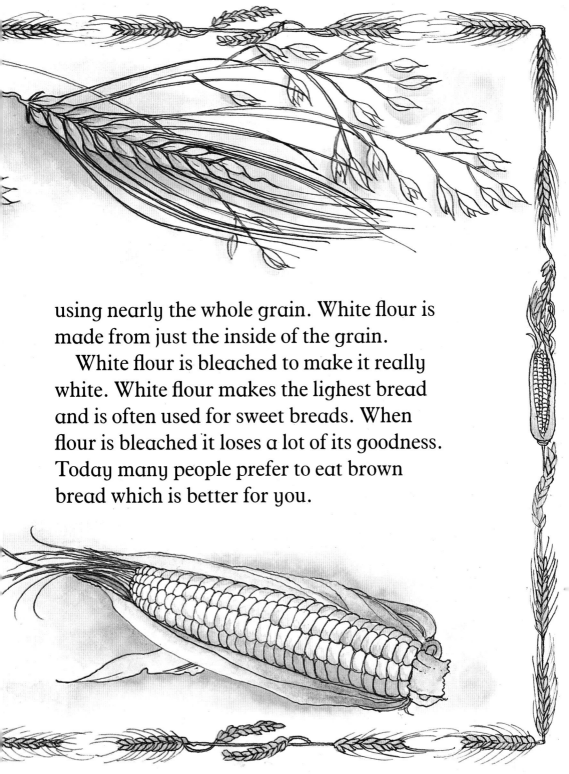

using nearly the whole grain. White flour is made from just the inside of the grain.

White flour is bleached to make it really white. White flour makes the lighest bread and is often used for sweet breads. When flour is bleached it loses a lot of its goodness. Today many people prefer to eat brown bread which is better for you.

All sorts of flour

Flour milled from rye, barley or corn and
even cooked rice and potatoes can all be used
to make bread. These breads all have a
distinctive flavour, texture or colour. Rye
bread is a very dark brown, almost black. It
has a strong taste. Corn bread is a beautiful
golden yellow and is best eaten fresh from the
oven. Rice and potato breads are surprisingly
light and moist. Loaves can also be made
from a mixture of grains which gives them a
combination of flavours and tastes.

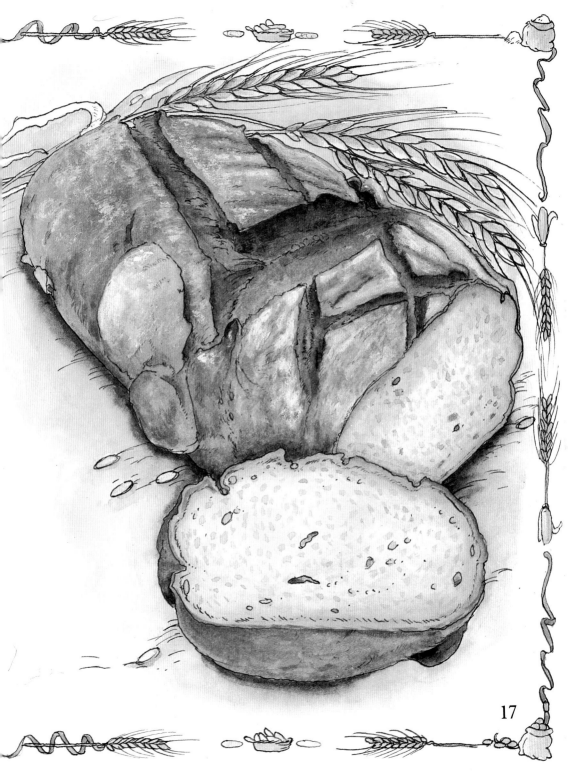

Shapes and sizes

Bread can be made in all shapes and sizes, ranging from small rolls to large loaves. White French bread is long and comes in different thicknesses. A 'baguette' is quite thick, but a 'ficelle' is very thin.

One of the oldest English shapes is the cottage loaf. These round loaves are made by cooking a small ball of dough on top of a big ball of dough. Loaves can also be made by plaiting the dough together.

In France a sort of bun called a 'croissant' is very popular at breakfast time. The name means 'crescent' in French.

Toast and sandwiches

Bread is eaten in lots of different ways all over the world. In many countries toast is very popular for breakfast. It is spread with butter and then something sweet like marmalade, honey or jam.

Bread is also often the main part of a meal. Hamburgers, hot dogs, and sandwiches are all made from bread. They come in all shapes and sizes with lots of different fillings. Bread can also be used to make sweet dishes, like bread and butter pudding, and summer pudding.

Pizza and naan

The main ingredient of pizza is bread. A dough base, usually made with white flour, is covered with a topping mixture. It is then put into a very hot oven and cooked all together. Favourite pizza toppings include tomatoes, cheese and herbs.

Naan dough is rather like pizza, but it is cooked without a topping. It is usually served with a hot curry and is particularly popular in India and Pakistan.

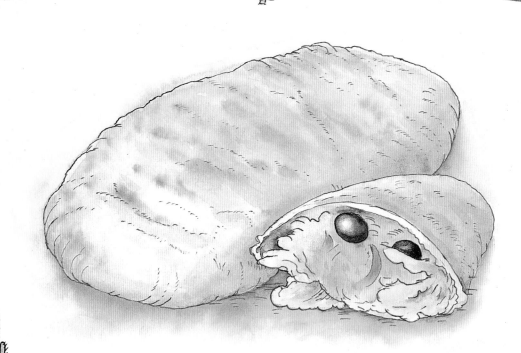

Pitta and tortilla

Pitta bread is made of leavened dough
cooked at a very high heat. In the oven the
bread rises and puffs up. When it is cooked
you can open it up to make a pocket. Pitta
bread is often served filled with meat kebab
and salad. It is very popular in Middle
Eastern countries, Greece and Turkey.

Mexican tortillas are made of maize flour, warm water and salt. The dough can be flattened by slapping it between your palms, or rolled with a rolling pin. Tortillas are often served as a snack stuffed with vegetables and spicy sauce. Tacos are tortillas stuffed with a meat filling and can be served as a main dish.

Bread for tea

Bread dough can be made sweet and rich by adding sugar, butter, fruit and eggs. Sweetened breads are eaten all over the world. The Italian kind is called 'pannetoni'. It is a dry bread with fruit in it. In Austria, Germany and Poland sweet bread cakes are called 'kugelhopf'. In Britain the most

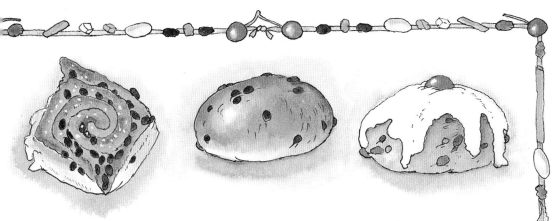

common sweet buns are currant buns with fruit in them and a sugary icing. They can be cooked as single buns or in a bun ring. Chelsea buns, which are filled with butter, sugar and fruit, are particularly rich and delicious.

'Tsoureki' is a special Greek Easter bread. It is plaited and then sometimes decorated with hard boiled eggs that have been dyed red. Almonds and sesame seeds are sometimes sprinkled on top.

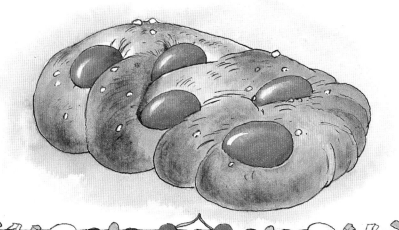

Index